BLIND BOONE

BLIND BOONE

PIANO PRODIGY

MADGE HARRAH

Carolrhoda Books, Inc./Minneapolis

Dedicated to the memory of Wayne B. Allen, music publisher, songwriter, friend. Also dedicated to Kayla, who loves books.

Acknowledgment:
I wish to thank Dr. Kenelea Johnson, Director of Outreach Services, New Mexico School for the Visually Handicapped, for her expertise and encouragement.

Carolrhoda Books, Inc.
A division of Lerner Publishing Group
241 First Avenue North
Minneapolis, MN 55401 U.S.A.

Website address: www.lernerbooks.com

Library of Congress Cataloging-in-Publication Data

Harrah, Madge.
    Blind Boone / by Madge Harrah.
      p.   cm. -- (Trailblazer biography)
    Summary: Presents the life and career of the blind pianist who toured the country after the Civil War, bringing ragtime and other African American music to the concert stage.
    Includes bibliographical references and index.
    ISBN: 1–57505–057–9 (lib. bdg. : alk. paper)
    1. Boone, Blind, 1864–1927—Juvenile literature. 2. Blind musicians—United States—Biography—Juvenile literature. 3. African American musicians—Biography—Juvenile literature. [1. Boone, Blind, 1864–1927. 2. Pianists. 3. Musicians. 4. Blind. 5. People with disabilities. 6. African Americans—Biography.] I. Title. II. Series.
ML3930.B597 H37 2004
781.64'56'092—dc21   2002153294

Manufactured in the United States of America
1 2 3 4 5 6 – JR – 09 08 07 06 05 04

CONTENTS

*John William "Blind" Boone defied the odds by becoming a
successful concert pianist in the post-Civil War era.*

AUTHOR'S NOTE

Many years ago, when I was a student at the University of Missouri in Columbia, I became friends with an elderly musician in town named Wayne B. Allen. One day Allen remarked to me with quiet pride, "I was Blind Boone's last manager."

"Who was Blind Boone?" I asked.

Allen looked at me in disbelief and exclaimed, "You don't know? Why, he was one of the greatest pianists who ever lived!"

"Tell me about him," I said.

On that day, I began to learn about the phenomenal African American musical prodigy John William "Blind" Boone. Blinded at six months, Boone became a concert performer at age fifteen. He played not only in cities but also in small towns and rural communities all over middle and western America, where professional entertainment was a rare treat. He played classical music and ragtime for farmers in overalls, women in homemade dresses, children who listened with awe to his music. He played for sophisticated audiences in Denver, Chicago, Boston, Washington, D.C., and other cities, receiving rave reviews. He toured for forty-seven years throughout America until his name became a household word.

Boone's fame was based on his concert performances, his compositions for piano, and his amazing ability to repeat any piece of music, having heard it only once. He is also ranked among the pioneers of ragtime due to his early ragged versions of African American songs. He was the first pianist to perform ragtime music on the concert stage in the United States and Canada. He also played spirituals, cakewalks, and other forms of music developed by African Americans. Those songs were usually played by black performers in bars and clubs. Had it not been for Boone, concert audiences might not have heard such music or given it credibility.

After Boone's death in 1927, his fame faded. His compositions that were published during his lifetime went out of print, and most of the piano rolls and recordings he made also vanished. If he had lived in the days of radio and television, his genius likely would have brought him international recognition and a place in the music history books.

When, as a children's book author, I speak in schools and mention Blind Boone, the children ask as I once did, "Who's that?"

So here is the story of Blind Boone.

Madge Harrah
Albuquerque, New Mexico

From the age of six months, little Willie Boone could not see the bright sun or his mother's face. He learned to use his other senses to explore the world around him.

GROWING UP BLIND

Three-year-old Willie Boone turned his face toward the warmth of the sun. He could tell from the way the heat hit his skin that the sun was getting low in the sky. Where was his mother? She'd said her errand would take only a short time. He twisted around on the bench outside the servants' quarters of the home of General Shed, where he and his mother lived. He picked up a spoon and a pan lid that he kept with him. Beating out a rhythm on the lid, he made up a song. He sang at the top of his voice, "Rachel Boone, Rachel Boone, time you're here, getting Willie Boone's supper!"

Soon he heard footsteps hurrying down the path—his mother's footsteps. He dropped the pan lid and the spoon and held out his arms. She swept him up and gave him a hug. He freed his hands and ran his fingers lightly over her familiar face, pausing to touch her closed eyelids and the roundness of the eyes beneath. Her eyelids fluttered beneath his gentle touch. Then he moved his fingers to his own face and pushed on his eyelids but they stayed closed. They didn't flutter the way his mother's eyelids fluttered nor was there any roundness underneath. His mother had told him many times how he had almost died with brain fever when he was six months old. She had told him how the doctors removed his infected eyes and sewed the eyelids shut in order to save his life. She told him he was blind.

Blind? What did that mean? he wondered.

She said that when she looked through her eyes, she saw trees and sky and clouds and people. They made colored pictures all around her. But she added that Willie didn't need to see to learn about the world. All he needed to do

Willie's mother, Rachel Boone, did not shelter her son just because he was blind. She encouraged him to venture out into the world.

was to listen carefully to the sounds around him and use his other senses, which were touch, taste, and smell.

Eagerly Willie explored his world, asking questions about the things he encountered. He learned to name the different kinds of birds from their songs. He knew the chirping of sparrows, the harsh squawk of crows, the cooing of doves, the liquid spill of the meadowlarks' song. He learned to identify the different kinds of animals from their smells, their feel, and noises that they made. He knew the bellowing of cows and the sweet, grassy odor of their manure. He recognized horses by their soft noses and high-pitched whinny. He knew the clucking of hens and the soft fur of kittens.

Rachel gave her son a long slender stick, which he swung back and forth to feel his way around as he memorized the different paths in the neighborhood. He learned the path to the outhouse, the big oak tree, and General Shed's barn. And he could find the path to Mrs. Cockrell's rosebushes, which had soft-petaled blossoms that perfumed the air but pricked his fingers with thorns.

When he went with his mother into the homes of the white people for whom she washed clothes and cooked, Willie sniffed, touched, and listened. He enjoyed the crumbly feel of fresh cornbread on his tongue and the tangy odor of boiling coffee. He liked the slick feel of the polished floors beneath his bare feet, the tinkle of the piano in the parlor, and the soft voice of Mrs. Shed as she explained to his mother the plans for the day.

He soon realized that every person he met had a special voice unlike anyone else's. Their footsteps were different, too. Some walked slowly with a heavy tread. Some scurried lightly along the paths or sidewalks.

Sometimes other children would try to sneak up on Willie. But he could never be fooled. "Oh, I know you!" he'd shout, calling out the person's name, whom he'd recognized from the rhythm of the stealthy footsteps. He laughed at the children's amazement.

As Willie grew a little older, his mother told him stories about her life in Kentucky, where she had once lived. Rachel had been born a slave. She was owned by descendants of Daniel Boone, a famous frontiersman who helped settle Kentucky. Rachel had heard of other slaves escaping to freedom in the North, where slavery was illegal. She had wanted to find a way to freedom, too. When the Civil War began in 1861, many more slaves began fleeing to states in the North hoping to find a better way of life. Sometime during this war between Southern and Northern states, Rachel decided to take her chances and run away.

Although there is no record of how she managed to escape, there is a good chance that she had the help of people on the Underground Railroad. This secret organization of white and black people across the country opposed slavery. Its members risked their own lives to help slaves escape to freedom. They provided hiding places and transportation for the runaway slaves who were making the dangerous journey north. There was an active Underground Railroad in Kentucky, and Rachel would have known about it.

Rachel told Willie of how she finally found her way to west central Missouri, near the small town of Miami. There she sought refuge in a Union army camp, a base for soldiers who were fighting for the North. Rachel worked for many months at the camp, cooking for the white soldiers. She did not say much to Willie about his father except to mention that he had been a bugler in the camp.

Willie liked hearing his mother describe how happy she had been when he was born in the camp on the morning of May 17, 1864. Many soldiers stopped by her tent to see the newborn baby that day.

Rachel told Willie that she soon decided an army camp was no place to raise a child. She took him to Warrensburg, Missouri, where she got work as a cook and washerwoman in the home of General Shed. She said that it was a Warrensburg doctor who saved Willie's life by removing his infected eyes. The North won the Civil War in April of 1865, she told him, and now all black Americans were free from slavery.

Black men, women, and children on the Underground Railroad sought shelter and hiding places among antislavery white families.

RECONSTRUCTION

Like many southern cities, Charleston, South Carolina, had suffered great devastation by the end of the Civil War.

When the Civil War ended in April 1865, the nation was left with many problems to solve. The North and the South had to reunite into one peaceful country again. The South had to rebuild and repair itself after the destruction of the war. And the country had to decide what rights African Americans should have and how those rights should be protected. To tackle these problems, President Abraham Lincoln had developed a plan to reconstruct the nation. This challenging time in American history became known as the Reconstruction period.

During Reconstruction, African Americans gained important rights. They were given full citizenship, and black men were given the right to vote. A handful of African Americans became government leaders and successful business owners. But many former slaves struggled to survive from day to day. Although Warrensburg remained relatively peaceful during the Reconstruction period, such was not always the case in other places.

Some white people believed that African Americans were inferior to whites. They did everything they could to hold black people down. The problems were especially bad in the South. White groups such as the Ku Klux Klan formed to terrorize black people with violence and even murder.

Southern landowners took great advantage of their black workers. The landowners needed black men, women, and children to continue working the land for them, but they didn't want to pay them. They used threats and violence to keep the workers from fighting for fair treatment.

After several years, the U.S. government stopped focusing on reconstruction and the rights of freed slaves. The Reconstruction period ended in 1877. Soon afterward, southern states took away many of the rights that black people had gained during Reconstruction.

In rural Georgia, a young person plays on a homemade fiddle.

Willie liked hearing his mother's stories. He was not sad about being blind. It was the only way of life he knew.

Warrensburg was a good-sized town of more than one thousand people. It was located in the middle of farm country about sixty miles southeast of Kansas City, Missouri. It was the county seat and drew people from surrounding farms and smaller towns. Two important buildings, the Johnson County Courthouse and the Davis Mercantile Store, sat across from each other on Main Street.

Willie loved listening in on the conversations between lawyers outside the Johnson County Courthouse in Warrensburg.

Willie liked going to town on errands with his mother. He enjoyed the noise and bustle of the busy crowds that gathered on Main Street throughout the week. He listened to the busy farmers who traveled into town to trade corn or eggs or chickens for flour and molasses. He heard lawyers discussing their cases as they gathered outside the courthouse. He listened to women calling to their children, dogs barking, and people singing and whistling. He liked the mixed odors of horse droppings, sweaty bodies, cigar smoke, and wet dogs. He enjoyed the taste of the peppermint drops the townspeople sometimes gave him.

But most of all he liked music, any kind of music. He loved the hymns that he heard in the Methodist Church, Colored, the name of the church he attended with his mother each Sunday. He also liked the spirituals that black men and women sang. These songs were from the time of slavery, and they were filled with both despair and hope. Other songs had lively rhythms that inspired people to clap as they sang.

Willie felt especially drawn to the piano. He often crept close to listen when the white children practiced their pieces in the homes where his mother worked. How he wished he could play those pieces, too! But there was no money for piano lessons, and Rachel couldn't possibly afford to buy a piano for Willie.

One day Willie heard a lively piano piece that he just couldn't resist. He moved close to the piano and asked what the piece was called. The girl playing it said it was "The Sultan Polka." Then she asked if he'd like to try it.

He climbed up on the bench and laid his fingers on the slick smooth keys. She showed him how to hold his hands and helped him pick out the melody. Then, to her astonishment, he played the piece with both hands all the way through.

Word spread quickly that little Willie Boone could repeat the pieces the other children played. Soon other families were allowing him to play their pianos.

When Willie was five years old, a man named Columbus Morrow gave him a tin whistle. Willie was delighted to have an instrument of his own at last. He began playing all kinds of tunes, adding variations that amazed his listeners. When Mr. Morrow gave him a harmonica, Willie began to play chords on it. Soon he learned that he could make interesting sounds, including a train's wailing whistle, a donkey's bray, a rooster's crow, the cluck of a hen, and the meowing of a cat. He composed new songs, sometimes playing into a teacup, which he shook back and forth to create a warbling sound.

Always outgoing, Willie loved to perform. He enjoyed the enthusiastic response of an audience. Then he landed on an idea. Why not start a band of his own? He found six other African American boys to play with him. The boys performed on Main Street near the Davis Store for the next several years, collecting money in a tin cup.

Later Willie recalled the experience in this way: "I organized a band of seven little boys at that time. I was the youngest and the leader of the band. We had two horns, two French harps, a drum and a comb. I was the teacup artist. When I was about nine the boys got mad and quit because they said I kept most all we made."

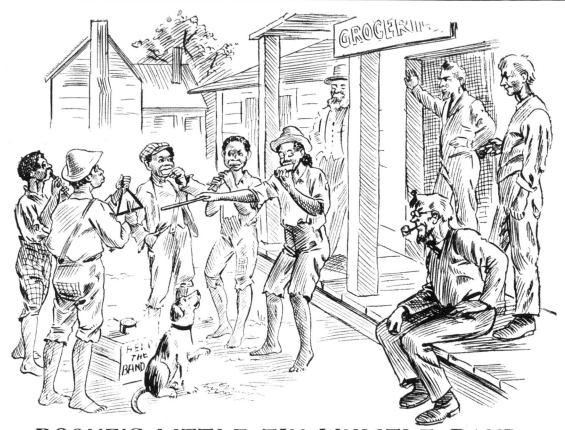

BOONE'S LITTLE TIN WHISTLE BAND

This caricature shows Willie (center) directing his first musical band.

When Willie was eight years old, his life changed. That year his mother married a man named Harrison Hendrix. Harrison had five sons: Sam, Ed, Tom, Harry, and Ricely. Willie had always wanted brothers and was happy about the marriage. Rachel and Willie moved out of General Shed's home to live with Harrison and his sons in their small log cabin. The cabin was located in a poorer part of

This small cabin was home to Willie, his mother, his stepfather, Harrison Hendrix, and his five stepbrothers.

town, where most African Americans lived. Willie found that he liked having five brothers and became close friends with Sam. He was glad that his mother had a husband to help care for her.

Around that time, another important change happened in Willie's life. A number of townspeople were talking about sending him to the famous Missouri School for the Blind in Saint Louis. They had seen his great musical talent and thought he deserved a real education and a chance to study piano. Rachel and Harrison couldn't afford the school's fees. Together, though, some of the white townspeople pitched in the money to pay for his schooling. "We want you to go and then come back and show Warrensburg what you can do," they told him.

The whole town soon got behind the plan to send Willie to school. State senator Francis M. Cockrell, whose home was in Warrensburg, arranged for the Johnson County court to provide railroad fare and money for expenses. The women of the town sewed new shirts and other clothing for Willie to take with him. Senator Cockrell contacted the head of the Saint Louis school and arranged for Willie to be admitted as a student for the upcoming term. Thomas T. Crittenden, a Warrensburg resident who later became governor, added his support.

In the fall of 1873, many well-wishers, including Willie's entire family, accompanied him to the train station in Warrensburg to see him off. They helped him onto the train and placed him in the care of the conductor. They instructed the man to see that Willie was delivered safely into the hands of an official from the school. The school official had promised he would be at the station in Saint Louis to meet Willie.

And so, harmonica in his pocket, walking stick in one hand and sack lunch in the other, Willie embarked on a great adventure.

As a port city, Saint Louis attracted people from all over the country and the world.

2

ADVENTURES IN SAINT LOUIS

The conductor led Willie to a seat and said that the trip to Saint Louis would take more than six hours. He told him that the toilet was in a small closet at the end of the car and promised to come back from time to time during the trip to check on him. As the conductor walked away, the train lurched with a clang and a shudder. Willie reached out, groping for something to hold on to. He grabbed the windowsill and felt the cold glass press against his knuckles. The train picked up speed, its wheels racketing against the tracks. Then it settled into a steady rhythm that pounded against Willie's eardrums. He took a deep breath and coughed as the harsh smell of soot

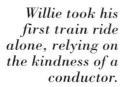

Willie took his first train ride alone, relying on the kindness of a conductor.

and smoke burned his lungs, and the swaying of the coach flung him back and forth in the seat.

Questions flooded his mind. He wondered what life would be like in the big city and if he would have trouble finding his way around.

In Warrensburg he knew every path, every fence. He knew the strong odor of mud and decaying weeds down by the creek, the clang of the anvil in the blacksmith's shop, the rasp of the grindstones in the mill near his family's small log cabin. All these things told him where he was as he tapped his way down the streets with his long slender stick.

He wondered what he'd do if the conductor forgot to help him off the train in Saint Louis. He'd heard Senator Cockrell tell the man to look after him. And he'd been assured that someone from the school would meet him at the station. But what if no one from the school showed up? He huddled in the seat, both anxious and excited as he tried to prepare himself for his new life ahead.

Now and then the porter walked through the coach, announcing the name of the next stop: Knob Noster, Sedalia, Tipton, California, Jefferson City. Each time, Willie listened anxiously. He heard the sound of passengers in his coach stirring around, banging luggage, and struggling past him down the aisle. This was followed by the noise of other people getting on. As the hours passed, Willie decided that they'd never reach Saint Louis. But at last the clacking of the wheels slowed, and the porter called, "Saint Louis! Union Depot!" The train shuddered to a stop like a dog shaking itself.

Willie got his first taste of Saint Louis at the city's large and crowded Union Station.

Willie felt greatly relieved when the conductor came and led him down the steps to the station platform. There a man from the school greeted him and shook his hand.

As the man guided him from the station, Willie turned his head from side to side. He listened to the chuffing breath of the idling engines, the calls of the conductors, the chatter of the passengers as they greeted friends or hurried to board the train. He heard the hiss of steam and felt a burst of damp mist against his face.

The mist changed into warmth, telling Willie that they had stepped out into sunshine. His mother had often described colors to him, explaining that the sun was yellow, strawberries were red, grass was green, the tablecloth was blue. He'd sometimes experienced a strange sensation in his head when he touched a particular color and sometimes he'd heard a tone. As he felt the heat of the sun on his skin, he heard a warm singing sound that caused his spirits to rise. The sound of yellow.

He and the man rode through the streets in a jouncing buggy behind a horse whose hooves clopped on the cobblestone streets. Other unfamiliar sounds, other smells, enveloped Willie in a rich cloud: smoke, sun-heated garbage, the shouts of street vendors hawking apples and cabbages. He also noticed patches of air that reeked of stale beer combined with snatches of music played on tinny out-of-tune pianos. Already he could tell that Saint Louis was much different than Warrensburg.

He and the man were met at the school by a woman with a pleasant voice. She explained that she was the school matron and helped care for the students in the school. When she asked his name, he replied, "John William Boone."

She welcomed him and led him around the school, introducing him as John to the others. He liked the use of his proper name, which marked for him the beginning of his new life. He would no longer be called by his nickname, Willie.

John learned that he was one of over a hundred blind students of all ages. Only six of these students were African American, but this did not bother John. He was used to spending time with white and black children and

MISSOURI SCHOOL FOR THE BLIND

At the Missouri School for the Blind, Willie became known by his first name, John.

being accepted by both. He soon made friends at the school, causing them to laugh with his imitation of birds and animals on his harmonica.

Any lurking doubts he might have felt over his new life vanished when he discovered the pianos in the music department. These pianos stood on the fourth floor of the school. Listening to the older piano students practice their pieces filled him with joy. He wanted to take piano lessons, too. But he was told he'd have to wait until he finished some of the basics, such as spelling, grammar, arithmetic, and geography. These subjects simply did not interest him. He sometimes skipped his regular classes and hid out near the piano rooms, hungry to hear new music.

He was particularly impressed by the piano playing of Enoch Donley, a white student who was a senior that year. Enoch played beautiful, complicated piano pieces unlike anything John had heard before. Enoch said it was classical music.

John listened with awe as Enoch played a piece called "Whispering Winds" by Hermann Wollenhaupt, a famous German composer. He could almost feel the breezes of spring brushing his face and ruffling his hair as Enoch's fingers rippled up and down the keyboard. When Enoch had finished, John approached him and asked if he could touch the keys, just for a minute. When Enoch agreed, John sat down and repeated a section of the music he'd just heard. It was Enoch's turn to be amazed.

John begged Enoch to give him private lessons. Struck by John's determination, Enoch asked the school administration for permission to do so. They agreed on one

During his practice sessions, John lost himself in the feeling of the piano keys under his fingers and the sound of the notes he played.

condition. Enoch and John had to promise to keep up with their regular studies.

Because all the practice hours were reserved for the older students, John had to practice on an old piano that was stored in the attic. Enoch saw that John had an unusual talent for memorizing and repeating difficult music. Still, he made the boy start from scratch. John went through the usual routine of finger exercises while also learning the proper placement of his hands on the keyboard. He learned the different intervals that make up chords and the time values of the notes: whole, half, quarter, eighth, sixteenth.

Enoch's insistence that John learn basic music theory and proper piano technique soon paid off. John could combine his natural talent for memorization with his newfound finger coordination. He was thrilled to hear the improvement in his piano playing.

In his spare time, John continued to repeat the pieces he heard other children playing. He also learned the complicated music that Enoch was practicing for his senior recital. John called his ability to learn music by ear "grabbing music."

Soon Enoch was bragging about John to his own piano teacher at the school. The teacher was intrigued. He asked to hear John play a piece of music.

On the day that John was to play his selection, the music teacher slipped into the room, unnoticed, just as Enoch asked John to begin. So perfect was John's timing, so expressive the playing, that the professor exclaimed to Enoch, "He's a genius."

Soon the superintendent of the school heard about John's remarkable musical talents. He began inviting John into his own home to perform for his guests. By the end of the school year, John had become a very capable pianist. He had also memorized a large list of piano pieces.

When he returned to Warrensburg for the summer, he was greeted enthusiastically by the residents. They were eager to hear him play the piano. They invited him to play for community activities and church socials. It was good to be home again, but John looked forward to another year of study in Saint Louis.

When he returned to school that fall, though, he found that everything had changed. Enoch Donley had graduated, and the school superintendent who had befriended John had been replaced by a different man. This new superintendent did not think black children should be treated the same way that white students were treated. Like many white people at the time, this man did not believe black and white people were equal. For the first time, the black students were denied many of the privileges that were allowed the white students.

The superintendent soon got word that John sometimes skipped his regular classes to practice the piano. Responding to complaints from John's teachers, the superintendent limited the amount of time John could play music. He also placed him in a broom-making class. The superintendent must have thought that learning to make brooms was a more practical skill for a blind black boy than learning to play classical music. John knew he was being treated differently because he was African American. He didn't like it one bit.

Learning to make brooms was not the education that John wanted. As the year progressed, he became more and more unhappy. He began running away from school to escape the boredom and sadness he felt there. For two or three days at a time, he would wander the streets of Saint Louis.

Saint Louis in 1874 was a lively, busy city. It was called the Gateway of America because people of different ethnic backgrounds passed through as they headed west for New Mexico or Oregon or Minnesota or Louisiana. The Mississippi and Missouri Rivers, which met in Saint Louis, carried multistoried steamboats that looked like frosted wedding cakes. There were also keelboats, rafts, and heavy barges loaded with coal or grain or lumber or livestock. Newsboys shouted, fire wagons clanged, trains wailed, steamboats hooted.

Travelers from all parts of the country stopped in Saint Louis.
The docks bustled with activity.

Often John would seek refuge in the Tenderloin District. This section of Saint Louis was known for its poverty and rough ways. But it was also the place where people went to hear good piano playing in the saloons and gambling houses.

How did John find his way to that part of town? Was he led there by someone he met on the street? Where did he sleep at night? No one knows. What is known is that he played his harmonica on the streets to earn money for food. He spent much of his time in the saloons on Franklin Avenue and Morgan Street. Sitting quietly in these bars, he listened to piano players pounding out lively versions of popular songs and black folk tunes.

They often improvised rhythms that had an unusual, ragged sound. It was wonderful music, which John had never heard before.

John loved the excitement of the city, the crowds, the noise. Most of all, he loved the music. But after a while he would get tired and hungry, and he'd return to the school where he would be punished for running away.

At the beginning of John's third year at school, the superintendent gave him a stern lecture. He must quit running away or he would be expelled. He would be allowed to play the piano once in a while *only* if he proved that he could obey the rules. Meanwhile, he was to continue making brooms.

John tried to behave, but he still did not like attending his regular classes. He certainly did not like making brooms. All he wanted to do was study music. A couple of times when he could stand school no longer, he slipped away for a day or two and romped on the streets. Each time the superintendent threatened to expel John if he didn't straighten up.

Things brightened briefly when the superintendent called John into his office and said that it was time for the school's annual concert exhibition. If John was a nice boy and did what he was supposed to do, he would be allowed to perform. The superintendent explained that a committee from the state legislature was coming for its yearly visit to the school. The committee members always checked on the school's progress and attended a performance of students with exceptional talent. Senator Cockrell from Warrensburg would be attending the concert this year.

The superintendent felt it would be good for John to perform. Thrilled, John promised to stay in school and go to class. He'd do anything he had to do to get to play.

John got to work practicing a piano piece for the concert. The piece was called "Charming Thoughts Schottische." It was a simple but pretty dance. When the day of the concert arrived, he played well and received praise from Senator Cockrell.

The performance had been wonderful, and now it was over. When would he have the chance to play again? John thought about running away for a while, but he didn't want to get into trouble. He worried that he would disappoint his mother and the people of Warrensburg if he flunked out of school. Instead of running away, John resolved to behave from then on.

For a while he did much better, but finally the lure of the streets proved too strong, and he ran away again. Hungry and dirty, he returned to the school after a few days. This time the superintendent made good on his threat and expelled him. Not wanting his mother to learn of his disgrace, John put off going home. He told the superintendent that he had a relative in Saint Louis with whom he could stay until his mother came for him. Then he once more took to the streets.

At last, overcome by hunger and loneliness, he made friends with a train conductor named Mr. Kerry. The kind conductor arranged for John to ride to Warrensburg for free in exchange for playing his harmonica for the passengers. Later, recalling that episode, he said, "I owe a lot to that conductor."

When John arrived home, he confessed to what had happened and tried to explain why he had become so unhappy at the school. He wasn't sure anyone would understand. To his great relief his mother forgave him. So did the townspeople. They were glad to have him back home.

Soon John found work as a musician. The directors of the Foster School, a school for white students in Warrensburg, hired him to play the piano for the children as they marched back and forth to their classes. Often he was asked to play for church services and community events. He also reorganized his old band, which performed at local fairs.

John was happy to be home, but he realized how crowded his family's one-room cabin was. It could hardly fit six growing boys and two adults. John dreamed of someday earning enough money to build a nice home for his mother. But he wondered how he could ever hope to make that kind of living.

He had just turned twelve when he met a smooth-talking white gambler named Mark Cromwell who devised a scheme that once more threw John's life into turmoil.

*When John Boone met sweet-talking Mark Cromwell at a
Missouri county fair, he had no idea how his life would change.*

3

KIDNAPPED!

John had finished performing at a fair in Warrensburg when Cromwell stopped him on the street. The man praised John's musical ability lavishly, telling him what a genius he was. Cromwell said he had never before met anyone so young with such talent.

Then he presented himself as a manager who could set up a concert tour for John that would bring in thousands of dollars and national fame. John was skeptical at first. He said that he received good money for his performances at county fairs, traveling circuses, and church socials. Cromwell snorted in disgust and said that was nothing. He promised additional riches, such as wonderful meals, train travel, fancy hotel rooms, and spending money for John's pocket. He even promised that John could have enough left over to send payments to his mother. Cromwell said he would mail the money to her each week. He said that John would end up so rich he could buy his family whatever they wanted.

John caught his breath. There it was, the answer to his dream! He was only twelve years old. But with the help of this white man, he could give his family the nice house they deserved. Right then and there, he agreed to go with Cromwell. But he needed to go home first to tell his mother what was happening so she wouldn't worry. There was no time for that, Cromwell said. He had an urgent appointment in another town, and they needed to leave at once. He said that he would write a note to John's mother explaining everything. She'd understand when she saw how rich and famous her son had become.

Rich and famous. Dazzled by the prospect of fortune to come, John hurried with Cromwell away from the fair.

Cromwell continued to lead John on with sweet stories as they headed out of town on foot. John had expected to ride the train, but Cromwell explained that train travel would come later.

Their first stop was the town of Holden, a few miles down the road. Cromwell told John to play his harmonica on the street. All the while, Cromwell collected the money people gave in appreciation of John's music. In Holden an African American man who knew John came up and tried to talk with him. Before John could say anything, Cromwell hurried him away. He led John into a back alley and out of town. At the next town, John again performed on the street and Cromwell collected the money. This continued from town to town. Where were the concerts that Cromwell had promised? John wondered. Where was his share of the earnings?

Day after day passed, and still none of Cromwell's promises came true. John became more and more suspicious the farther they got from Warrensburg. Soon Cromwell began going into saloons and spending the money on gambling games. He insisted that John play his harmonica in the saloons to make even more money, all of which Cromwell kept for himself.

Weary and frightened, John realized that Cromwell had never written to his mother. He knew she must be worried sick. Maybe she even thought he was dead.

Whenever John tried to talk with Cromwell about the broken promises, he got put off with excuses and lies. Later the fame and fortune would come, Cromwell told him. All they had to do was hit it big in a couple of

Men such as Cromwell spent hours in saloons such as this one, gambling away what little money they had.

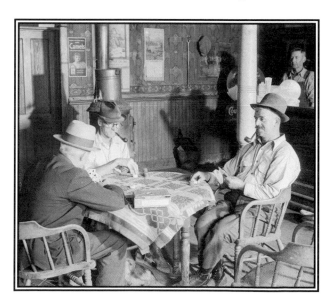

games. Once they had enough money, Cromwell would be able to set up the tours he had talked about. Wait, just be patient, all would come right, Cromwell said

If John persisted in his questions, Cromwell tried to calm him by giving him candy and praising his talents. If John continued to ask questions, Cromwell beat him. He said that he owned John and the boy must obey him. By then John was so afraid of Cromwell that he didn't try to break away or seek help from other people. Even if he had tried to tell someone his story, no one would believe an African American boy over a white man. Cromwell could easily convince people that he had a right to this child.

John had no way of knowing that Rachel and Harrison were desperately trying to find out what had happened to their son. They'd heard a couple of rumors that John had been seen traveling with a white man, but they did not have any firm leads. They asked people from Warrensburg who were traveling to visit friends in other towns to inquire if anyone there had seen a small blind boy.

Dragging John farther and farther from home, Cromwell worked his way on foot across central Missouri. There were no train rides, no lavish meals, no fancy hotels as he had promised. There were just nightly card games in dingy saloons. Sometimes a saloon had a beat-up piano, tinny and out of tune. Then John would play his own variations of traditional and new African American songs. He tried out the rhythms he had heard in the bars in Saint Louis.

One night in Columbia, Missouri, Cromwell got into a game of chance called Seven Up with a man named Sam

Columbia, Missouri, was one of many stopping points for John and Cromwell during their rushed tour.

Reiter. Having gambled away all his money, Cromwell wagered ownership of John as if he were a piece of property instead of a human being. In the end, Cromwell lost John to Reiter. John thought briefly that he would be safe. His hopes were dashed when Reiter took him home and locked him in the attic. Reiter kept him a prisoner for three days. Finally, at John's pleading, Reiter let him out to play and get some fresh air for a little while in the backyard.

Cromwell was lurking near Reiter's home, hoping to steal John back. After a while, Reiter went into the house and left John alone. Cromwell grabbed John and whisked him away. He paused only long enough to disguise John as a girl. John feared he would never be free.

Rachel and Harrison had not given up on finding their son. At last they learned that John was in Cromwell's clutches and that the two had been seen near Columbia. Harrison set out in pursuit. Making inquiries along the way, Harrison finally caught up with the pair near Vandalia, Missouri. As soon as he tracked them down, he demanded his stepson's release.

John was relieved to hear the familiar voice of his step-father. He could hardly wait to go home. But Cromwell,

John was finally rescued from Cromwell's clutches near Vandalia, Missouri.

still the smooth talker, told Harrison that he had great plans for John's career. He convinced John's stepfather to allow him to take John to Vandalia, where he said he had scheduled a concert. Harrison finally agreed but did not let them out of his sight during the trip. He told Cromwell that as soon as the concert was over he was taking his son home.

It soon became clear to Harrison that Cromwell had no intention of giving the boy up. Finally John's stepfather asked for help from the police. Free at last, John returned with Harrison to Warrensburg and the welcoming arms of his mother and brothers.

John was glad to have escaped from Cromwell's cruelty. But he found that his friends liked hearing the stories of his adventures. He started to see the drama he had just lived through as being exciting and unusual. Life in Warrensburg was peaceful but slow. John was often filled with a desire for more adventure. Maybe Cromwell had been right about one thing. Maybe he could make a living as a musician. Besides, he told himself, his family's cabin was still overcrowded and money was scarce. Perhaps his parents would be relieved if he struck out on his own.

*Being blind didn't dampen John's dream of becoming a
successful musician.*

NEW HORIZONS

John knew that musicians sometimes rode the trains playing for passengers and collecting money. He decided to try this out for himself. He began riding the Missouri Pacific trains back and forth between Sedalia and Jefferson City in Missouri. Along the way, he performed on his harmonica for the passengers and received generous tips. He then teamed up with two other boys, Tom Johnson, banjo picker, and Ben Franklin, harmonica player. The threesome performed together on the trains for many months. They added to their route the Chicago and Alton train line from Jefferson City north to the Missouri towns of Mexico and Glasgow.

Sometimes John and his bandmates stopped and performed in towns along the route, sharing a room in a cheap hotel. John liked to stop in a town on most Sundays to attend church services. Sometimes he was asked to play the piano for the congregation. He did this with enthusiasm, adding his own embellishments to the hymns he remembered from his childhood.

As outgoing and friendly as ever, John enjoyed meeting new people on the trains and in the towns along the way. In his spare time, he entertained restless children with his harmonica imitations of birds and animals. Travel-weary parents always seemed grateful for this diversion.

John had been traveling on the trains for more than a year when things fell apart. When the three boys first started riding the trains together, they had no problem with the conductors. Musicians were often allowed to travel for free as long as they entertained the passengers. But as time went by, more and more traveling entertainers, candy salesmen, newsboys, and beggars began hopping the trains. Sometimes they badgered the passengers and made a nuisance of themselves. After a number of passengers complained, the railroad companies made an announcement. Anyone boarding a train had to pay full fare. Begging and selling in the aisles had to stop.

By then the boys had begun fighting with each other, and their friendship was breaking up. When they'd first started out, they had pooled their tips each evening and divided the money evenly. The time came, however, when John realized that he was getting far larger tips than the other two. He suggested that they stop dividing the money and that each one keep for himself what he earned. The other two said that wasn't fair. After the railroad announcement, they got into a heated argument about how to divide the money.

John finally said, "I will not travel with you boys anymore. I know the most anyhow. I can go alone."

John was determined to make something of himself. He knew that he could no longer travel on the trains, but he was not content to return home.

He decided to go to Glasgow, Missouri. He had stopped in this town before and played in an African American church known as the Colored Methodist Episcopal Church. Once in Glasgow, John contacted his friend the Reverend Mr. Jeffries, pastor of the church. He hoped the pastor would give him a job. The Reverend Mr. Jeffries remembered John's musical talent. The pastor arranged for John to play the piano regularly for his church services. He even offered John a place to stay.

Most people in Glasgow had never heard a pianist who could play the way John could. His fame began to spread throughout the town. The slightly-built blind boy with the engaging smile became well known. It was said that he could copy any piece he heard, adding variations of his own that rippled up and down the keyboard like wind over water.

The Reverend Mr. Jeffries was intrigued by John's remarkable talent. He asked John if he could promote him as a musician. John quickly agreed. The reverend took him on a concert tour in Iowa. Over a period of three months, John would perform in African American churches throughout the state.

He enjoyed the trip and hoped that it would give him extra money to send to his mother. But John soon learned that an unknown black musician was not a great attraction. It wasn't easy to encourage people to come to his concerts. In the end, the cost of the tour was greater than the money earned from the concerts. John and The Reverend Mr. Jeffries were forced to abandon their tour and return to Glasgow.

John went back to playing in the local church, and word of his talent continued to spread. The Reverend John Lee, minister of the Colored Methodist Episcopal Church in Fayette, Missouri, was one of the people who had heard about John. He wondered if the young musician would come to his church to play at services there. Both John and The Reverend Mr. Jeffries agreed that it might be a good idea. They were right. People in Fayette flocked to hear John play, and he became friends with many young people in the church and community. If only he could find a way to attract such audiences in other towns and cities.

One day, John received an invitation to come to Columbia, Missouri. John Lange Jr., a prominent black businessman in Columbia, had heard about John. He invited him to perform during a weeklong Christmas festival. The festival was sponsored each year by the Second Baptist Church. John accepted the invitation. His spectacular performance during the festival created a sensation among the listeners.

Lange took a liking to the friendly and talented fifteen-year-old boy. At thirty-nine years old, he and his wife Ruth, had no children of their own. They wondered if John would like to live with them. That way they could sponsor him and help him develop his talent. The Reverend Mr. Jeffries realized by then that he lacked the time or money to launch John in a career. He agreed to let John live with the Langes if he liked the idea. John was thrilled by Lange's offer. He gladly chose to move to Columbia. With Lange's belief in his talent, John's hopes for a career in music rose once again.

John trusted Lange from the beginning. He knew that Lange respected him and would not take advantage of him, as Cromwell had. And he soon learned that Lange

John Lange Jr. became an important father figure to young John Boone.

knew firsthand how to make something of himself as a black man.

Born a slave in Kentucky in 1840, John Lange had been the second of sixteen children. After African Americans were freed from slavery, he had worked in his father's butcher shop. He went on to become a contractor and built all but one of the roads that existed in Boone County. He also built the first black Baptist Church in Columbia and was known for his generosity to worthy causes in the community. John knew that such success for a former slave was unusual. He could tell that Lange was not afraid to step out and take chances.

Ruth Lange, a kind woman, reminded John of his own mother. Devoted to her home, she sometimes took care of nine-year-old Eugenia, her husband's youngest sister. John enjoyed playing with Eugenia and also with Ed, Ruth Lange's pet parrot, which had a temperamental nature and a colorful vocabulary.

Excited by Lange's plans to help him build a career, John wanted to share with his mother the news of what was happening. The Langes bought him a round-trip train ticket so he could go home for a brief visit. His parents and brothers greeted him with joy, delighted to see him and hear his news.

John brought with him a contract for his mother to sign. It said that Lange was forming the Blind Boone Concert Company and that John would become a full partner in the company when he was twenty-one. Lange also promised to send Rachel Boone ten dollars each month. John was thrilled that he could give money to his family.

When John returned to Columbia, Lange began looking for opportunities for him to play in the Columbia area. All the while, he considered ways to launch John's career with a bang. "You have great things in you, my boy," he would say. "Listen to me and I'll help you stand where you belong."

One day Lange heard that a famous black pianist called Blind Tom was coming to Columbia to give a concert. He was doing what few African American performers had ever done. He was performing regularly in concert halls for black and white audiences. His musical ability impressed his listeners.

A painted portrait of pianist Blind Tom

BLIND TOM

Thomas Green Bethune had been born a slave in 1849 and was owned by a man named General James Neil Bethune. He grew up on a plantation in Muscogee County, Georgia, with his mother and father. As Tom grew older, it became obvious that he was mentally impaired. He could not care for himself or travel alone. He could not keep up a simple conversation, although he could repeat speeches he memorized. He resisted taking baths. Sometimes he leaned over and swept endless circles on the floor with his hands. Today he might be diagnosed with a condition called autism.

But from early childhood, he showed a remarkable talent as a gifted musician. When he was four, he was brought to a music store in Columbus, Georgia, where he heard a music professor play an original composition. Tom sat down and repeated the music note for note. By the age of five, he was composing music of amazing originality.

Promoted by General Bethune, Tom began traveling and performing when he was nine years old. During his many years as a professional pianist, Tom composed many original piano pieces. One of Tom's most famous compositions, "Battle of Manassas," was based on descriptions of the battle that he heard during the Civil War. Tom also composed music based on the sounds of nature, as did Boone. But unlike John William Boone, Tom did not have a manager who treated him fairly. Tom's earnings went straight into General Bethune's pocket, even after the Civil War freed Tom and his parents from slavery.

Lange learned that Blind Tom's Columbia concert would include a challenge to local pianists. Any pianist would have a chance to try to outplay him. At each of Blind Tom's concerts, Tom's manager would call for a local pianist to come to the stage and play a piece of music, which Tom would repeat. Tom would then play a different piece, often one of his own compositions, which the challenger would be asked to repeat.

Right away Lange saw the chance to gain the recognition for John that he'd been looking for. So far as Lange knew, no one had ever successfully met Tom's challenge. He believed that if anyone could, it might be John. He could just see it. Two blind pianists competing against each other. One would be only fifteen and the other would be more than twice that old and already famous— what an opportunity!

He told John his idea, and the two of them began making plans for the big night.

Blind Tom regularly attracted large crowds to his performances.

5

THE CHALLENGE

The concert took place in Columbia on March 3, 1880, in Garth Hall, which later became the Haden Opera House. Word had gotten out around town that John Lange's young star was going to challenge Blind Tom. The auditorium was packed that night. White listeners sat on one side of the room, black listeners sat on the other. People not only filled all the seats on the floor but also the gallery and part of the stage. A stagehand who was a friend of Lange's managed to seat Lange and John in chairs backstage near one of the wings.

Blind Tom was led onstage, and the concert began. John could sense that the brilliance of Tom's playing astonished the audience. Tom's performance of his difficult and inspiring composition, "Battle of Manassas," was especially powerful. At last it was time for the challenge. A music teacher from Christian College in Columbia played a piece for Tom to imitate. He performed it without a flaw. However, the teacher was unable to repeat what Tom played to challenge her.

Then John's big moment came. Lange led him onstage and introduced him to Tom and the audience. When people realized that the time had come for their local favorite to challenge the master, excitement ignited the crowd.

John played first, a piece called "Butterfly Gallop." This song contained many fast-moving notes and trills that fluttered over the keyboard like the flight of a butterfly. Then John sat back and listened as Tom performed the piece. He played it perfectly.

It was Tom's turn to play something. He performed a long, difficult piece called "Delta Kappa March." As tension mounted in the room, John sat down and repeated the entire piece without a single mistake. The audience went wild. "Give him the chance and John can be as great as Tom!" they yelled.

John and Lange were thrilled over the success of the concert. They hoped it would give John the respect he needed to begin a career as one of the few black pianists in the country.

Lange arranged for John to study piano at Christian College. A teacher there gave John several weeks of intensive training in piano techniques. The teacher also taught him classical pieces by famous European composers such as Bach, Beethoven, Liszt, Chopin, Brahms, and Wollenhaupt, as well as the American composer

Louis Moreau Gottschalk. Like John, Gottschalk was part African American.

John was already familiar with most of those composers because of his lessons with Enoch Donley back at the Missouri School for the Blind. He was particularly fond of Wollenhaupt's "Whispering Winds" because it brought back memories of his friend. His favorite composer of all, however, was Franz Liszt. This Hungarian pianist and composer created music that embraced the entire keyboard with sweeping runs of notes and dramatic chords.

While John attended lessons at Christian College, Lange organized the Blind Boone Concert Company to promote John's talents. He chose as their motto, MERIT, NOT SYMPATHY, WINS. He wanted to stress John's musical ability rather than his blindness.

After the creation of the Blind Boone Concert Company, John's name underwent another transformation.

John loved the dramatic beauty of music written by European composer Franz Liszt.

Just as young Willie became John when he left home to go to school, now John became Blind Boone to most people. He began to go by the name Boone, as if that were his given name. Even his friends began calling him Boone.

Lange and Boone started on their first tour that summer. Boone had high hopes for the tour, despite gloomy predictions from Lange's friends. "Within six months you'll be dead broke and will come to town pushing that boy in a wheelbarrow," one of Lange's friends said. No one believed people would pay good money to see an unknown black pianist.

Boone played throughout towns in Missouri. Sometimes he and Lange traveled in horse-drawn wagons rented from livery stables. Sometimes they traveled by train. They carried a piano with them since not all communities had pianos. When traveling by wagon, they tied the piano down with ropes and covered it to protect it from dust and rain.

Since there were no radios or televisions then to broadcast advertising for the concerts, Lange and Boone had to advertise in a different way. They sent letters to newspapers ahead of time to announce their arrival and put up posters once they reached town. Sometimes, acting like a barker in a circus, Lange stood on the town square and called out information about the concerts to the people passing by.

During that summer, Boone found time to do more than perform. He also worked on new music of his own. One day he learned about a horrible event that inspired him to compose a beautiful composition. He was practicing the piano when Lange burst into the room and said, "I just heard some terrible news. A tornado has destroyed Marshfield. They say over a hundred people have been killed."

The enormity of the tragedy pressed down on Boone like a heavy weight. Knowing that they were due to travel to the town of Marshfield soon for a concert, he asked, "What do we do now? Do we still try to go there?"

Lange replied that the concert might lift people's spirits. He said he'd send a telegram to see if they still wanted Boone to come. It was a good thing they carried a piano with them on their tours, since there probably wasn't an undamaged piano left in Marshfield.

Lange then opened a newspaper and read aloud the survivors' eyewitness accounts of the storm. Boone learned that it had happened on a Sunday evening when many people were in church. The building exploded from the force of the storm, and the roof fell in and crushed the people who were caught underneath. Stores, houses, and barns were destroyed. Trees were uprooted. Livestock had been killed. The only building left untouched, said the report, was the courthouse.

A man had once told Boone about a tornado he had experienced. He had described how he'd watched a line of dark clouds roll out of the southwest and form a funnel. The funnel writhed like a snake toward the ground and roared forward with a sound like a freight train.

Boone had held snakes so he understood writhing, and he'd certainly listened to the roar of freight trains. And wind. Yes, he knew wind, the way it swirled leaves and dirt into the air, stinging his skin. But a tornado had to be a thousand times worse than that.

Turning back to the piano he placed his fingers on the keys. "I imagine it went this way," he said.

He began to play, creating thunderous passages to convey the terrible devastation brought about by the storm. When he finished, Lange said, "Play that again, Boone." Boone did, adding to the piece to heighten the effect.

The people of Marshfield sent word that they did indeed want Blind Boone to come. He decided to premier "Marshfield Tornado" during his performance there.

The concert took place in the courthouse. Nearly all the survivors came seeking solace and diversion after their tragedy. They crowded into the courtroom to hear Boone play.

Saving his new composition for last, Boone ran through his usual list of songs to the enthusiastic response of the crowd. Then came the moment for his grand finale.

The destructive power of a tornado inspired Boone to compose music that imitated the sounds of the storm.

He began with chiming chords that sounded like bells calling people to church. He followed the chimes with variations on a hymn to imitate the sounds of a church service. Suddenly he slammed his hand down on the lower keys to suggest the crash of thunder. Playing with wrists, elbows, fists, forearms, fingers, he swept up and down the keyboard to create with music the rising wind and clanging of alarm bells. He played rumbling chords that grew louder and louder to imitate a funnel cloud sweeping down upon the town. He slammed his open palms on the low keys to suggest the collapse of buildings. He played strange wailing sounds on the high keys to create the cries of frightened people. Then the noise of the storm died away, and he softly tapped a piano key over and over, like water dripping among the ruins.

Lifting his hands from the keyboard, Boone realized that the cries hadn't stopped. Puzzled, he listened to a rush of footsteps retreating from the room. He asked what was happening. Lange said that his music had been so lifelike that it made the people relive the tornado.

Boone was dismayed to hear that he had frightened his audience. He and Lange talked it over and decided to donate the profits from the concert toward rebuilding the town. Boone wondered if he should leave out "Marshfield Tornado" from future concerts. But word about his amazing composition spread to other communities, and they began requesting the piece. Like Blind Tom and Gottschalk, Boone had become one of the few African Americans to perform his own music for concert audiences. He was making his way as both a pianist and composer.

Fifteen-year-old John Boone at the beginning of his budding concert career

6

THE EARLY YEARS

Boone's summer tour with Lange lasted for three months. They returned home briefly to rest and to sell stock in the company to partners. The partners invested money in Blind Boone's concert career in exchange for a share of the profits.

With this additional funding, Boone and Lange headed out again for another round of concerts. This time they included in their company an eleven-year-old African American singer named Stella May. Lange's wife, Ruth, went along to act as chaperone. Lange and Boone had hoped that adding a singer to the company would attract larger audiences. They soon discovered, however, that they could not yet afford to travel with four people. Ruth and Stella May ended up going home.

Boone's fame mostly spread through word of mouth. Newspaper stories and glowing concert reviews also helped him along. He welcomed any chance to show off his piano playing and earn more fans.

Boone and Lange came home that summer to rest. Then in September of 1881, they began their second year of touring. Their ticket sales had improved so much that they asked Ruth Lange and Stella May to rejoin the company. Concert audiences responded with enthusiasm to Stella May's beautiful voice. She sang spirituals and folk ballads that reflected the unique culture of African Americans.

Ruth brought Ed the parrot along in his cage. Ed delighted Boone. He enjoyed hearing the pet parrot talk.

For thirteen seasons in a row, Stella May lent her vocal talents to Boone's performances.

Lange with
Ed the talking parrot

Ed also served as a source of entertainment to the children in the towns where the company stopped to perform. Once, a woman and her young daughters asked Lange if the parrot would sing for them, but Ed refused, saying, "I ain't well, I'm tired." Another time Ed escaped and flew to the top of a pole. When the members of the company begged him to come down, he yelled, "I don't have to."

One of their stops that fall was Kansas City, Missouri. Here Boone was invited to demonstrate pianos for J. W. Jenkins & Sons Piano Company during a fair. The piano exhibit took place in Floral Hall, a large building on the fairgrounds. After getting Boone settled at one of the pianos, Lange told him to stay there until he returned. He then left to go find a newspaper reporter to come and hear Boone play.

While Lange was gone, a fire broke out in the hall. Boone smelled the smoke and heard the commotion but later said that he decided not to "run foolishly." After all, he didn't know the way out. He was certain that Lange would return for him. He forced himself to remain calm and continued to play the piano even as the smoke thickened.

Guided by the sound of the piano, Lange found Boone and led him from the building just as the roof collapsed. Only then did Boone understand how close he and Lange had come to dying. He realized once again how lucky he was to have John Lange by his side.

By his third year of performing, eighteen-year-old Boone was known throughout several midwestern states, including Iowa and Illinois. The advance agent's advertising attracted bigger and bigger crowds. Those who heard Boone play told their friends and relatives about his amazing talent and urged them to attend his concerts. They wrote letters about him to friends who lived in other towns and spread the word about him when they traveled. Newspapers printed feature stories about the young musical star, and music critics published positive reviews.

Boone impressed people wherever he went. He knew how to match his musical talent with charm and good humor on stage. Still a natural showman, John loved inspiring an audience. Sometimes he laughed out loud with enjoyment when his listeners stamped and cheered after he had performed a particularly difficult number. He often performed in small rural communities. In these small towns, any kind of traveling entertainment was a novelty and was therefore welcomed by the people. He played in

Admirers surround Boone at a railroad station during a concert tour.

tents, schools, churches, courthouses, lodge halls. He usually played for audiences filled with both white and black audience members. But in most cases, the black and white listeners sat separately.

Boone included the challenge in each of his concerts, which increased local interest. He was always able to repeat the music note for note, including the mistakes that the challenger sometimes put in to trick him.

Sometimes the challenge piece was unusually long, and Boone worried he might bore an audience if he repeated the whole thing. Then he would select key passages to repeat. He would stop sometimes to explain to the audience how the composer had developed the various themes. His goal, always, was to entertain. He was extremely sensitive to any sounds that signaled restlessness in his listeners. If he thought he was losing their attention, he immediately switched directions in order to get them involved.

Boone loved to please an audience, but he also wanted to please himself. He liked many different kinds of music, from classical European pieces to African American songs and compositions. He performed them all for his audiences.

He usually performed classical music in the first half of a concert. He knew that many members of his audience would not have been exposed to this type of music. Often he started a performance with a showy piece, such as Chopin's "Military Polonaise" or Liszt's "Hungarian Rhapsody No. 6." "You got to hit that music critic right between the eyes, get his attention," he said. He knew a good review would help spread his name

In the second half, he said, "Now let's put the cookies on the lower shelf where everyone can reach them." Then he played his own elaborate arrangements of hymns and popular tunes, music that was familiar to both black and white listeners. Reflecting the influence of his favorite composer, Liszt, he strung together soaring melodies, rich chords, and dazzling strings of notes. His fingers rippled up and down the keyboard and made music that sounded like the strumming of a harp. To please the children, he did imitations on the piano of various sounds, which he called "Drummer Boy," "Gospel Train," "Country Man Tuning Fiddle," "Drum and Fife," "In-coming Train," and "Music Box."

During this second half of the concert, he also played his own arrangements of African American songs. He knew that many white audience members would not be familiar with the sounds he had heard as a child in Warrensburg and Saint Louis. It was music that had mostly been played by black musicians in churches, homes, and saloons. Some people didn't respect it or expect to hear it in a concert setting. But that didn't stop Boone.

As he played, he imitated the sounds he had heard as a child in the Tenderloin District. Often he used regular rhythms in the lower notes and the syncopated, or "ragged," rhythms in the high notes. Another popular form of music developed by African American musicians was the cakewalk. Cakewalks were a popular form of dance and entertainment. While the music played, people strutted in a circle, performing difficult and unusual steps. The person who was judged the best won a cake. That music, too, found its way into some of Boone's concerts.

Boone was delighted to find that his revolutionary concerts were a success. His audiences loved them, loved him, and crowded around him afterward to express their admiration.

Children and adults participated in popular cakewalk contests. Here, a group of youngsters prepare for the dance.

JOHN LANGE, Manager

BOONE'S COMPOSITIONS.

1. Waltz De Concert No. 1, Tarentella.
2. Waltz De Concert No. 2, Caprice Africaine No. 1.
3. "Sparks" Gallop De Concert . . . . . Africaine No. II. Gavotte Chromantique. "Spinning Song." Woodland Murmurs. "Serenade." "The Whippoorwill" Romance, Josephine Polka.

"REVERIES."

1. The Spring. 2. Echoes of the Forest. 3. Humming Bird.
"TRANSCRIPTIONS WITH BOONE'S VARIATIONS."
Nearer My God to Thee. My Old Kentucky Home. Old Folks at Home. "Nicodemus." Melodie De Negres.

SONGS.

"Cleo," "Dinah's Barbecue," "You Can't Go to Glory that Way," "When I Meet that Coon To-night," "Wha' Shall We Go?" "Signs of the Times," (Words by Dunbar, music by Boone.) "Georgia Melon,"—Boone. "You Can't Make It Win at the Gate," "The Melon Season is Over," "Dat Morning in The Sky," "That Little German Band," "Thanksgiving Turkey," "That Only Chicken Pie."

Boone's financial success allowed him to spend money on elegant concert programs.

A Concert Career

On Boone's twenty-first birthday, Lange made him a full partner in the concert company. He would have more control over company decisions, and he would receive a large share of the profits. Boone traveled to Warrensburg to tell his mother the good news. She responded with joy and pride to hear how successful her son had become. Boone, too, was grateful for everything he had. He had come a long way from his days of poverty in Warrensburg.

By this time, Boone and his company had settled into a routine. They traveled for ten months a year, returning home to rest over the summer. During the touring months, Boone often played six or more concerts a week, with time off only on Sundays.

Boone loved the adventure of traveling, just as he had when he was a boy. Being a successful concert pianist gave him the chance to visit and explore cities such as Denver, Des Moines, and Chicago. Even the smallest towns interested him. He often helped the advance agent plan the routes of his concert tours. While the agent searched the maps with pencil and paper, Boone would recall the most insignificant villages on their proposed routes. When sitting in large depots that he had previously visited, he could tell Lange which train was coming in just by the sound of the train's bell.

Sometimes the Blind Boone Concert Company returned to towns where Boone had played before. People who had heard him in the past came back to hear him again, bringing friends and relatives from surrounding areas. Crowds of people often met Boone at the train station to greet him and shake his hand.

Boone had an uncanny ability to remember almost everyone he ever met on tour. He could recognize someone as soon as he or she spoke. If a person said to him, "I met you when you were here before," Boone could then call that person by name just from the sound of the voice. He also remembered anyone who had played a piece of music for him as a challenge. Many times he would sit down and repeat the music they had played without being reminded what it had been. For Boone the pleasure of being with people was almost as great as the pleasure of playing music.

He particularly enjoyed the children he met on his tours. He sometimes showed them his gold watch, which had been made for him in Switzerland. The lid of the watch was elaborately decorated with sculpted flowers, vines, and the profile of a horse framed in a horseshoe that was set with seven diamonds. The watch, which cost one thousand dollars, was a symbol to Boone of his success. He carried it everywhere he went.

Boone liked to tease children by telling them his watch could predict the future. Just before the national presidential election in the fall of 1888, a group of boys came up to Boone and Lange on the street. Boone opened the lid of the

Boone's unique gold pocket watch

watch and told them to look at the face. It showed not only the time but also the phase of the moon and the day of the week. When Boone pushed a button, the watch chimed the time. Boone then said, "Another thing it tells me, boys, is that Harrison is going to be our next president."

One of the boys later reported that they were amazed when Benjamin Harrison did indeed defeat Grover Cleveland in the election. After that, the boy and his friends firmly believed that Boone's watch had predicted the future.

Boone thrived on the adventure of touring and performing, but he welcomed the summer months when he could relax in Columbia. At home Boone practiced the piano every day. He learned new pieces and continued to compose songs of his own. He admired the way the classical composers developed their themes, weaving melodies and chords together in a colorful tapestry of sound. This was reflected in many of his original compositions.

Boone's reputation as a talented composer got around. One day Boone met a man who bet the pianist that he couldn't compose a piece on the spur of moment based on three notes selected at random. Boone bet he could. The man then played an F, A flat, and A natural. Boone sat down at once and played a lengthy piece all the way through, using those three notes as the theme.

When Boone finished the man said, "Bet you can't play it again."

Boone played the piece exactly as he had played it before. He called it the "Last Dream Waltz," and it became a regular part of his concerts.

His neighbors in Columbia, especially children, often gathered beneath the windows of Boone's piano room to listen to him play. He asked the children he met about their interests and encouraged them to fulfill their dreams.

He also talked freely about his lack of sight with them, telling them that he considered his blindness helpful to him as a musician. He said that it forced him to concentrate upon, and to remember, even the smallest differences in the sounds around him.

Boone also liked to surprise children and adults with what he said was his ability to "see" color through touch. People reported seeing Boone announce the color of someone's clothing just by feeling it. Once, a woman in Columbia said he asked her permission to touch the sleeve of her dress. She said he felt the material and correctly told her that her dress was patterned with pink flowers. Another time, a red-haired child said that Boone touched her hair and said, "Oh, this is a little red-headed girl, isn't it?"

Boone said that certain musical tones also made him sense colors. He said, "To me red is the fiery note; blue, not quite pure, and white is like a clear liquid tone. Then there is yellow, the golden and glorious note, and black, the dismal and melancholy."

Sometimes his ability went even further, as if he were able to tap into information he read in other people's minds. A newspaper reporter said he was once startled when Boone accurately described the man's physical appearance without being told anything about him. Boone called this "seeing with my mind."

BOONE *and* COLOR SENSATION

One story about Boone's ability to sense color occurs in the memoirs of Maggie Banta Maddox, who wrote about meeting Boone in Polo, Missouri, when she was a child:

Blind Boone

One day Blind Boone came to town with his piano and his parrot. Our Opera House was over a store. Some men had to carry his piano up the stairs that were on the outside of the building. We kids got to watch. The parrot sat on top of the piano and said, 'Let her go,' with each step they made. Blind Boone sat outside the store and we gathered around him. He could tell what color our dresses were by feeling of the material. We got to go to his concert that night and it was just wonderful. We had two good musicians in town and they played some difficult pieces that Blind Boone had never heard before, but he sat right down and played them. All he needed was to hear them once.

Music was at the center of Boone's life, but he also cherished his time at home in Columbia for another reason. It gave him a chance to be in Lange's sister's company. Eugenia had always welcomed Lange, Boone, and Ruth home, eager to hear about their adventures. She sat for hours, listening to Boone practice. And she read to him each day from the newspapers.

Over the years, Eugenia had grown into a fine young woman. Boone realized that his feelings for her had deepened into love. In 1889, when Boone was twenty-five and Eugenia was nineteen, he proposed to her. She accepted, and they were married in October of that year.

Eugenia was a wonderful wife, supportive in every way. She continued to read the newspapers to Boone. She also read books on geography and American government, subjects Boone had rejected as a child. He listened enthusiastically, wanting to learn as much about the world as he could.

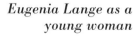

*Eugenia Lange as a
young woman*

Although Braille had been developed by the time Boone went to school in Saint Louis, he never learned to use it. Instead, he relied on his amazing memory, absorbing the details of everything he heard. He knew the names of the various politicians and the districts they represented. Not only could he name all the states and their capitals but also the counties in those states. He stored up a wealth of knowledge on many subjects that he could draw upon at will. His friends called him their "walking encyclopedia."

On Boone's next concert tour, Eugenia began accompanying her husband. Ruth Lange was delighted to have Eugenia's help. She had taken over the difficult job of keeping the accounting books and handling other business for her husband during their travels. Eventually Eugenia became treasurer for the company.

The Blind Boone Company was earning more money than ever. In the first year of his marriage, Boone found that he had enough savings to buy a home for himself and Eugenia. They decided to have a house built to their

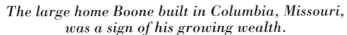

The large home Boone built in Columbia, Missouri, was a sign of his growing wealth.

Boone's pride, his Chickering grand piano

liking. It was a two-story house on Fourth Street in Columbia. They lived in this home during the summer months between tours.

In that house, Boone kept a nine-foot Chickering grand piano and an Edison Amberola phonograph, an early record player. He also had a Knabe player piano. This kind of piano was made to play by itself. Boone listened to the player piano in order to learn new music.

Boone enjoyed having the money to buy nice things for himself. At five feet tall and more than two hundred pounds, he always dressed well and looked attractive in his shirt, vest, tie, and suit. He also enjoyed buying and

Boone took great care with his appearance. He dressed in well-made suits and often wore fancy jewelry and a gold medal that Lange and Eugenia had given to him on his birthday.

wearing jewelry. Along with his gold watch, Boone bought and wore a platinum ring set with an enormous diamond. He also owned several other pieces of jewelry that were given to him as gifts from Eugenia and Lange. And he used a silver-headed ebony cane to help him find his way through a strange building or along a street.

With Boone and Eugenia settled in Columbia, Lange and Ruth moved to Kansas City. The couples often visited back and forth, traveling between Columbia and Kansas City on the train. Lange owned a huge touring car, which had a top that folded down. Boone enjoyed riding through the streets of Kansas City with the wind blowing in his face.

John Lange, Boone, and Ruth Lange in Lange's touring car

While taking the train to Kansas City, he sometimes stopped to visit his family in Warrensburg. Of all the purchases Boone made, he was proudest of the home he could finally buy for his mother. It was the fulfillment of his longtime dream. He continued to help his parents and brothers in any way he could.

Boone searched to find other ways to help the people around him. Looking back on his life, he saw many examples of kindness set for him by others. He remembered how the townspeople in Warrensburg had sent him to school and how the Reverend Mr. Jeffries had given him a home in Glasgow and taken him on tour. And, of course, he could never repay the efforts and sacrifices of his manager and friend John Lange. Lange had once said, "I have lost all I had more than once, trying to make Boone a success, but I'm proud today that I stuck with it."

Boone began donating money to repair churches and schools for African Americans in the Columbia area. Soon he was joking that he'd reroofed more churches than anyone else in town. He also gave money and encouragement to people in need. Boone was blessed all his life by the love and support of others, and he knew it. He welcomed the chance now to lend others a helping hand.

Jno. Lange and Jno. W. (Blind) Boone

The distinguished duo of Lange and Boone in the early 1900s

8

Ragtime
and Jim Crow

Sometime in the 1890s, Boone's touring took him across the ocean to Great Britain. While there he performed in England, Scotland, and Wales. He even met a member of the royal family. Back in the United States, his popularity stayed strong as he continued to tour with the Blind Boone Concert Company. He was riding high on all of his successes.

In 1901 Boone's beloved mother died of an illness. Four months later, his stepfather passed away. Those losses threw Boone into a period of intense grief. In his parents' memory, he bought four acres in Warrensburg and presented the land to his brothers. His only request was that the brothers not let the land go out of the family.

Over time Boone recovered from the loss of his parents and moved on with his life. His career continued to flourish. Stella May traveled with the concert company for thirteen years until her voice failed. She was followed by a series of other fine female singers.

By this time, Boone was known to a wide range of listeners across the country. His fame had spread not only to average Americans looking for entertainment but also to educated music lovers thirsting for live performances of classical music.

As the popularity of Blind Boone grew, so did the popularity of African American music. From the beginning of his career, Boone recognized the importance of black music as part of the American culture. He believed it deserved the same respect that European music had earned. He continued to play songs usually performed only in cheap saloons and dance halls. Boone's listeners, white and black, welcomed Boone's performance of music inspired by African American culture.

While Boone was performing black folk music in concert halls, other black musicians were performing similar music in clubs and saloons. Popular black musicians in Missouri experimented with ragged rhythms and used traditional African American songs and cakewalks as the basis for new compositions. This led to the growth of the movement that was finally labeled "ragtime." An African American composer named Scott Joplin helped put ragtime on the map with popular ragtime songs, called rags.

SCOTT JOPLIN *and the* GROWTH *of* RAGTIME

Scott Joplin was born to former slaves in Texarkana, Texas, in 1868. He became the most famous of all ragtime performers and composers, writing popular songs such as the "Maple Leaf Rag."

In the 1890s, he wrote groundbreaking piano pieces while living in Sedalia, Missouri, and performing at the Maple Leaf Club. Then in 1899, he met a white music publisher named John Stark. Stark recognized the importance of ragtime as a unique form of American music. He published

Scott Joplin

some of Joplin's songs, making ragtime available to the general public. Joplin continued to publish popular rags. Yet he died penniless in 1917.

Joplin's compositions influenced both black and white composers during the ragtime era. Ragtime produced many great artists, including James Scott, Scott Hayden, Arthur Marshall, and Jelly Roll Morton, to name a few. Their music found its way into clubs, saloons, and homes. But it was rarely respected as a serious form of art.

For years after Joplin's death, he and ragtime music were all but forgotten. In 1973 a Hollywood movie called *The Sting* featured some of his rags. The film brought Joplin and his songs once more to the attention of the American people. Ragtime is considered one of the great forms of American music.

Boone liked ragtime music and composed some ragged music of his own. In 1892 he had written a lively piece that was termed a "dance," but it was more like an early rag. Since then he had composed two other elaborate pieces called "Southern Rag Medley #1: Strains from the Alley" and "Southern Rag Medley #2: Strains from Flat Branch." These pieces became early ragtime classics. Another composition, "Camp Meeting Medley #1," also contained surprising rhythmic changes with overtones of rag. His compositions gave many concert audiences their first taste of early ragtime music.

Boone was friends with at least one other ragtime artist and composer, James Scott. In August of 1904 Boone was in Scott's hometown of Carthage, Missouri, giving concerts. He arranged to meet with the composer at a local music store.

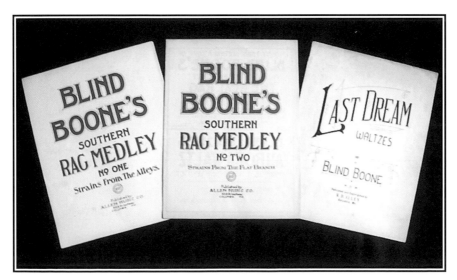

During the heyday of ragtime music, Boone composed some of his own early rags, which were published by Wayne B. Allen.

When Boone arrived at the store, Scott turned on a gramophone record of John Philip Sousa's band, a popular group of white musicians. Scott began improvising an accompaniment to Sousa's music on one of the store's pianos. Delighted, Boone joined Scott at the piano and played a melody on the high notes. The sound imitated a wind instrument called a piccolo. A crowd gathered in the store to hear these two famous men performing together. It was just the kind of spontaneous situation that Boone most enjoyed.

He was happy to share a free concert with fans of ragtime. But he did not like being exploited by greedy people who tried to take advantage of him. One summer when he was back in Columbia for a rest, a local music store owner invited Boone to come to his store. He said he thought Boone might like to try out a new piano that had just arrived. When Boone got to the store, he found it filled with customers the store owner had lured in by advertising a free Blind Boone concert. Angered, Boone left that store and went to a music store owned by Wayne B. Allen. Allen was a local white businessman and songwriter who also published sheet music.

When Allen heard what had happened, he locked the doors of his store to keep out the crowd and put a Closed sign in the window. Allen told Boone to play for as long as he wanted. He promised to see that people left him alone. Grateful for the solitude, Boone spent the rest of the afternoon in Allen's store, playing the different pianos. That was the start of a long friendship between the two men.

Throughout his life, Boone had formed friendships easily with people from many different walks of life. He had paid little attention to racial or social barriers. As a famous musician, he had avoided the harsher kinds of racism that many African Americans experienced on a daily basis. He also knew he had been lucky to live in towns that had treated him with kindness. In Columbia, Boone was recognized and respected as one of the city's "famous sons."

Boone had mostly been treated well on his tours, too. Until the turn of the century, Boone and Lange had been able to eat meals on the trains and find hotels or rooming houses in most of the towns they visited. In most towns, they could stay in relative comfort. However, they visited some places where they had to find rooms with private individuals in the neighborhood where African Americans lived.

But as the nineteenth century came to a close, Boone noticed the situation begin to change. In 1896 the United States Supreme Court had ruled on a case known as *Plessy v. Ferguson.* In this case, the Court said that segregated, or separate, areas for black and white train passengers were lawful. This decision had opened the way for further segregation in restaurants and hotels throughout the country. Since then many states had begun passing "Jim Crow" laws, named after a stage character that showed a black man in a negative light. These laws required black and white people to use different restrooms and drinking fountains. In some towns, African Americans were no longer allowed to stay within the city limits overnight.

Among other restrictions, Jim Crow laws required separate drinking fountains for black people and white people.

Restaurants and hotels that had welcomed the members of the Blind Boone Concert Company in the past began turning them away. The dining cars on trains refused to serve them, and they had to start carrying their own food. Segregated seating was strictly enforced in many concert halls. Some towns even insisted on two separate concerts, one for black listeners and one for white listeners.

Once, Boone and his company came close to canceling a concert because they could not find anywhere to stay in a town. In 1904 the company revisited Paola, Kansas, where they had been well treated in the past. This time they were denied admission to the hotel. They knew they would have to find accommodations elsewhere, but where could they go? They were scheduled to give a concert that night, and they were tired and hungry.

Boone posed for many portraits throughout his career.

On advice from the hotel clerk, they contacted an elderly African American widow at the edge of town. She took them in and provided them with beds and meals, but she would accept no pay for her hospitality. When Boone learned that the woman owed $350 on her home, he paid it off and presented her with the deed to the house.

Boone and his company were determined to keep touring. They dealt with the discomforts as best they could. They continued to make good money and to receive outstanding reviews in newspapers wherever they went, including cities in the South. Boone did not allow prejudice and mistreatment to dampen his desire to please a crowd.

Neither did Boone and Lange allow negative attitudes of others to change the fair way they treated the people they met. They hired James Shannon White, the grandson of Lange's former slave owner, to work for their company as an advance agent. The relationship was friendly and lasted for eight years before White left to start his own business.

Boone also refused to let the challenging times stop him from embracing new opportunities. In 1912 he became possibly the first black pianist to make piano rolls. These rolls were used in player pianos. Player pianos played music by themselves. They had become very popular throughout the country. They brought piano music into homes even when family members themselves did not know how to play.

To make a piano roll, a pianist played a special recording piano. Eighty-eight little carbon markers made marks on a revolving drum of paper as the keys were depressed. This became a preliminary master roll. The next step was to have a worker manually cut out the marked spots on the roll with die punches. Then the roll could be threaded into

The process of making piano rolls was complex and delicate.

a player piano. When the piano was turned on, the automatic mechanism inside responded to the holes in the paper. This caused the piano keys to play as the roll turned.

Boone signed a contract in 1912 with a piano roll business in Chicago called the QRS Company. The contract said that he would record solely for QRS for the next five years. Both Boone and Lange had hoped to do well financially with money from the piano roll sales. But the QRS Company did not make good on its contract agreement to give Boone a share of the sales. Boone later sued the company and was granted a small sum of money but not the amount he felt he was owed.

Boone sued QRS partly out of pride rather than a need for money. During the height of his career, his company sometimes took in four hundred to six hundred dollars or more for a single concert. That added up to big money in those days.

Ruth no longer traveled with the company. Sometimes Eugenia stayed home, too. During one of those times, Boone received a telegram saying that Eugenia was dangerously ill back in Columbia and might have to have surgery. The company canceled the tour and took a train to Kansas City, intending to catch the train for Columbia there. In Kansas City, they found that the last train to Columbia had already left. Lange asked train officials to send a special train of two coaches. The railroad company gave the right-of-way to Boone and company so they could finish their trip home. Boone had once begged rides on trains as a young performer. Now he rode in style in his own chartered coach. But all Boone cared about was

Eugenia, here with Boone, supported her husband during good times and bad.

getting home to his wife. Fortunately, Eugenia recovered, much to Boone's relief.

For Boone his family was more important than anything else he had. He loved Eugenia both as a wife and a friend, and he admired Lange above all other men. When Lange died in 1916 at the age of seventy-five, Boone was heartbroken. He experienced a period of spirit-shattering grief, both personally and professionally.

The two men had traveled together, worked together, and experienced hardship and triumph together. They had been not only business partners but also best friends, brothers-in-law, and father and son. And no one believed in John the way his manager had. Lange once said, speaking about Boone, "As an entertainer I believe him to be the greatest man on earth." With John Lange gone, Boone thought his career might be over.

Boone continued to perform as the ragtime era came to a close.

9

THE FINAL YEARS

With the encouragement and support of Eugenia, Boone slowly pulled himself together. He took over management of the Blind Boone Concert Company but soon realized he needed help in handling the bookings and the business details. The singer with the company at that time was Marguerite Day. She and her husband, John Day, offered to take on the task of helping run the company.

Boone was grateful for the help, but he knew it would not solve all of his problems. He was no longer as popular as he had once been. His concerts were attracting smaller and smaller audiences. People had access to motion pictures, phonograph records, piano rolls, and radio. Live performances were not as appealing with all those other options. The music Boone played was not as popular, either. Ragtime had begun to go out of style. Younger musicians were beginning to play a new kind of music called jazz. Boone did not play or like jazz. He called it "foolish talk."

Bookings for the Blind Boone Company became increasingly difficult to obtain. Most of the concert tours over the next three years took place in the midwestern United States. Once more Boone performed in schools and churches rather than opera houses and large concert halls.

Things changed briefly for the better during the 1919-1920 season. The company toured the eastern United States for an eighteen-month period, playing in many of the larger cities. Boone spent two weeks in Washington, D.C., a month in New York, a month in Boston, Massachusetts, and he performed at Harvard and Yale universities. Famous European composers Sergei Rachmaninoff and Ignace Paderewski heard Boone play during this tour and praised his talent.

Boone was pleased by the reception he received in the East, and he and Day made plans for another eastern tour. But in 1922, John Day died in an accident. Boone tried to carry on with the help of a businessman in Columbia.

The man promised to keep Boone's concert career going strong. But first, he said, Boone would need to sign some papers. He said the papers were just a matter of business. Boone couldn't see the papers, but his friend Wayne B. Allen could. Allen saw that the papers were actually checks for large sums of money and deeds to much of Boone's property.

THE JAZZ AGE

Jazz got its start with African American musicians living in New Orleans, Louisiana, in the early 1900s. These musicians took the ideas of ragtime to a new height, adding more complicated melodies and rhythms. They also used a variety of instruments. Drums pounded out rhythms that made people think of African dances. Trumpets and cornets blared notes that caused listeners to jump with surprise. Clarinets and saxophones tootled up and down the scales, spinning the melodies off in unexpected directions. The music was sassy and bold.

By the 1920s, jazz had replaced ragtime as America's favorite music. African American artists in cities all over America embraced the new music, as did many white musicians. Recording companies began making jazz records. Radio stations broadcast live performances by jazz artists. The motion picture industry even included jazz music in their movies. The decade became known as the golden age of jazz or the Jazz Age.

Allen decided to put a stop to the cheating. He went to the man's office and leveled his pistol at the man's heart, saying, "You've known me all your life and you know I mean what I say. Either you tear up those papers or I drop you where you stand." The man tore up the papers. Then Allen went to Boone and said, "Don't sign another thing until I've read it first." Boone was grateful to Allen for taking action. He asked his friend to be his manager, and the two men worked together from then on.

Boone and Allen decided that Boone might have a chance to earn a better living if he tried making piano rolls again. Boone's piano roll contract with the QRS Company had long since expired. Allen and Boone traveled to Chicago to try to get a new contract with another company. On the day of Boone's scheduled audition, he and Allen went to the building that housed the company's studios and offices. They arrived only to learn that the studio managers had already hired a man from California.

Allen left Boone downstairs and went up to confront the managers. He said, "I don't care who you've hired, I have a man with me who can outplay anyone in the world."

They said, "Prove it."

Allen wrote out a check to the company for a thousand dollars and said, "If this man can't do everything I've claimed, this check is yours."

Allen went downstairs and told Boone what was happening. Boone had charmed hundreds of audiences with his piano playing. He knew he could do the same thing now. He and Allen went upstairs together, and the managers brought in the man from California to challenge Boone. The Californian played first, a long difficult piece that he had composed. When he had finished, Boone applauded politely. Then he walked unassisted to a second piano in the room. He had located it from hearing the faint overtones given off by that piano's vibrating strings. He said, "That was very good. Here is the part I liked best."

Without even sitting down, Boone accurately repeated the whole middle section. The Californian leaped to his feet and rushed to shake Boone's hand, crying, "My God, I'd go to hell and back for this man."

The company hired both men. The next day, Boone played "Marshfield Tornado" for the rolls. He pounded with wrists, elbows, and forearms to create the crashing of the storm, as he always did. And he dragged his fingers up and down the keyboard so quickly that the tiny punches had no time to mark the individual notes. The mechanism jammed and had to be repaired.

Boone knew then that he'd never be able to record his most famous composition. He'd already given up on trying to get it written down. There was no way to mark the sound effects he used to create the storm. He said then that the piece would have to die with him.

Boone ushered in 1926 by performing a New Year's Eve program on KFRU, a radio station in Columbia. The program brought more responses from listeners than any previous program.

Feeling ill, Boone gave his last concert in Virden, Illinois, on May 31, 1927. He ended his program with the

"Marshfield Tornado." He was diagnosed by an Illinois doctor as having dropsy, which was probably related to heart failure. The doctor ordered Boone to go home to Columbia to rest. As the summer progressed, Boone experienced increasing weakness and shortness of breath. Requests for future concerts kept coming in, and Boone made plans to resume his career as soon as he regained his health.

In the fall, he thought of going to Hot Springs, Arkansas, for treatment. But he first decided to travel to Warrensburg to visit his stepbrother Sam. He died in Sam's home on October 4 and was buried on October 7 in Columbia in the cemetery near his and Eugenia's home. As a tribute to Boone's productive life, Marguerite Day sang the spiritual "I Done My Work."

During his lifetime, Boone toured for forty-seven years and performed in forty-four states, Canada, Mexico, and the British Isles. During his touring years, he wore out sixteen pianos. Although he continued to perform until just a short time before his death, he never did regain the status that he had experienced when he was younger. Gradually his savings had melted away as the earnings from his concerts dwindled.

Eugenia died two years later and was buried beside her husband. The graves went unmarked for many years, but in 1971 concerned citizens in Columbia raised the money to provide a headstone. It is inscribed with Boone and Eugenia's names.

Boone's accomplishments stand as a testament to his genius and enthusiasm. Born to a runaway slave, blinded at

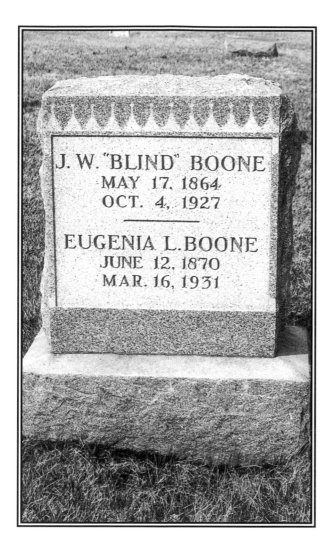

Boone and Eugenia's shared tombstone rests in the Columbia Cemetery in Columbia, Missouri.

six months, brought up in poverty, he had many obstacles to overcome. But he embraced life with vigor and went on to achieve greatness not only as a gifted musician but also as a courageous, generous man.

Lange's motto for the Blind Boone Concert Company was indeed well chosen:

MERIT, NOT SYMPATHY, WINS

Boone at his beloved grand piano

SHARING BLIND BOONE'S STORY:

A Postscript from the Author

Long before writing was invented, history was passed on from one generation to the next by storytellers. They memorized stories of events from the past and repeated those stories around their campfires so that everyone could learn and remember what had happened before them. Before the storytellers died, they trained other storytellers to take their place.

Even today people share their personal memories when they get together for holidays and reunions. The older people say, "I remember when I was young . . ." and they spin stories about the past. That is called oral history, and that's how I first learned about Blind Boone.

It was the winter of 1953. I was twenty-one and a music student at the University of Missouri in Columbia. I played both the piano and the violin. When the neck on my violin broke and needed to be glued, I asked a teacher where to go to get it fixed. She told me about an elderly man named Wayne B. Allen who had long retired from his career as a music store owner and music publisher. She said he still had a workshop in a loft downtown where he repaired broken instruments.

On a cold, snowy day, I climbed the stairs to the loft and knocked at the door. When a voice called, "Come in," I entered and stopped in amazement. I felt as if I had stepped into Santa Claus's workshop at the North Pole.

A man with white hair and a cheery smile stood beside a workbench holding a broken guitar. Other guitars, along with violins, banjos, and mandolins in various stages of repair, were strung on a long wire on the wall behind him. Snow and sleet hissed against the windows on either side of the workbench. When I asked Mr. Allen if he could repair my violin, he said yes, but I'd have to leave it and come back in a few days.

When I returned, Mr. Allen showed me the huge room where he kept over a dozen old-fashioned pianos and melodeons, left over from his days as a store owner. He smiled his appreciation when I played Chopin's "Military Polonaise" on one of his pianos. He said it reminded him of long ago when he had been Blind Boone's manager. That's when he told me his first stories about Blind Boone.

We became friends, and I returned often to play his pianos and listen to more stories about Boone. I started taking notes as Mr. Allen talked. There were no tape recorders or video cameras in those days. There weren't even ballpoint pens. I wrote notes in pencil on scraps of paper, the backs of envelopes, and finally in notebooks. These were not formal interviews but oral history recited by an old storyteller to a girl who was two generations younger.

Allen told me personal stories of his long friendship with Boone, dating back to the late 1800s. He also told me stories that Boone had told him about his childhood in Warrensburg, the Missouri School for the Blind, his kidnapping by Mark Cromwell, his rescue by his stepfather, the composing of "The Marshfield Tornado," his travels with Lange, and his concert tour in the British Isles.

BLIND BOONE was born in Miami, Saline County, Missouri, in the Federal Camp, in 1864, Seventh Militia, his mother being a contraband, cooking for the soldiers. He lost his sight from brain fever when six months old. His first instrument was a tin whistle, on which he could play any ordinary air after once hearing it. Next he was presented with a mouth organ by which he charmed the whole neighborhood—children coming from far and near to hear him. He soon became the favorite of all who knew him, and visited the best families in Warrensburg, where he then lived. (His home at present is Columbia, Mo.) People formed such an attachment for Boone that he was sent to the St. Louis School for the Blind to learn a trade and to be educated. This, however, was a failure.

Once hearing a pupil in the Institute practicing on the piano, he left his work, and stole to the piano, as it was impossible to keep his fingers off the keyboard. He soon became able to finger out several pieces, and it was impossible to keep his mind on anything else. He was dismissed from school and wandered around St. Louis, making his living by playing on a mouth organ, and such instruments as he could get his hands on. Conductor A. J. Kerry seeing the pitiful condition of the boy, put him on the train and sent him to his mother. He soon organized a little company and started on the road, tramping and beating his way from town to town. His company consisted of a player on each, a tambourine, a tri-angle and mouth organ, by which they gave concerts on the streets. He was not successful, however, and endured many hardships. A colored gentleman, John Lang, of Columbia, Mo., taking a liking to him, put him in the Sunday School to play for the children. He also made a contract with his mother to educate him in music and put him on the road. He has been very successful in pleasing his audiences, this being his twenty-seventh season.

Boone is an agreeable gentleman to meet. He likes to form acquaintances. Once having met a friend, he never forgets him; never forgets a voice; never forgets the pressure of a hand. He delights in recognizing persons after once meeting them. We will be pleased to have you meet him, if you wish, after the entertainment. He is always pleased to meet his friends.

JOHN LANGE, Manager.

Headquarters, 912 Park Ave., Kansas City, Mo.

PROGRAM

[Miss Emma Smith, our Soprano, a Kansas City girl, is a graduate of Lincoln High School. This is her sixth successful season with the company.]

Miss Emma Smith
Sixth Successful Season

Grand March Military	Wollenhaupt
Whispering Winds	Wollenhaupt
Camp Meeting Song	Boone
Military Polonaise	Chopin
Aurora Waltz	Boone
Plantation Song	Boone
Selection from Martha	Transcription Sidney Smythe
Humorous Song	Boone
Selections from El Trovatore	Gottschalk
Selection	Miss Emma Smith
Rhapsodie Hungraise	Liszt
Selection	Miss Emma Smith
Marshfield Tornado, descriptive	Boone
Imitations of various instruments	
Finale—"National Airs."	

STAFF

BLIND BOONE	*Uncle Thaw marriage*	PIANIST
JOHN LANGE	*Bro. In Law*	MANAGER
MRS. JOHN LANGE		SECRETARY
MRS. J. W. BOONE	*wife as Boone aunt*	TREASURER
MISS SADIE ROBNET	*My Sister in Law*	ASSISTANT TREASURER
MISS EMMA SMITH		SOPRANO

*Primary sources such as this concert program
helped bring Boone's story to life.*

Allen, who had at the age of eight attended the challenge match between Boone and Blind Tom, also described in vivid detail the excitement and shouts of the crowd that night. He showed me boxes filled with music that he had published, including music by Boone. I played Boone's music while Allen leaned against the piano and listened with a distant look in his eyes. When he died in 1955, I grieved at the loss of a valued friend.

In 1960 the Blind Boone Memorial Concert committee was organized in Columbia for the purpose of setting up a concert in Boone's honor, and I served on that committee.

During that project, I met people who had known Boone and Allen, and that's when I heard more stories about them both. In 1961 I wrote an article about Boone that was published in a national magazine, and I later wrote other articles.

I've continued to do research on Boone through the years, reading hundreds of old newspaper stories,

Sculptor Ai Qiu Hopen works on the clay model for a large bronze statue in memory of Blind Boone for the Blind Boone Park in Warrensburg, Missouri.

magazine articles, concert reviews, letters, program notes, cemetery records, and copies of obituaries. Many of these documents are stored in special archives in Columbia and Warrensburg. I've visited museums where items from his life are housed. I've listened to stories about Boone told to me by elderly people who heard him play, including some of my relatives. I've talked many times with Dr. Kenelea Johnson, my friend who works with the visually handicapped, about the ways in which people with limited vision learn to cope. She is also the one who explained to me that the ability to "see" color through touch and to "hear" color through tones is a recognized scientific fact.

Now I am the elderly storyteller sharing tales about Blind Boone with others, including you.

Pass them on.

CHRONOLOGY

1864   John William Boone is born to Rachel Boone on May 17. His eyes are removed six months later.

1865   The Civil War ends. African Americans are freed from slavery. Reconstruction begins.

1868   Scott Joplin is born in Texarkana, Texas.

1873   John is sent to the Missouri School for the Blind.

1876   John is expelled from the Missouri School for the Blind.

1877   John is kidnapped by Mark Cromwell. Reconstruction ends.

1878   John joins with two friends to perform for tips on Missouri trains.

1879   John meets John Lange Jr. in Columbia, Missouri.

1880   John outplays Blind Tom in challenge match. He and Lange form the Blind Boone Concert Company and begin touring. John, now called Boone, composes "Marshfield Tornado."

1886   James Scott is born in Neosho, Missouri.

1889   Boone marries Eugenia Lange.

1894   Scott Joplin first arrives in Sedalia, Missouri, home of the Maple Leaf Club.

1896   United States Supreme Court upholds segregation on trains in *Plessy v. Ferguson*. Racial discrimination grows throughout the country.

1899   Scott Joplin's "Maple Leaf Rag" is published.

1901 Rachel and Harrison Hendrix die in Warrensburg.

1908 Boone's "Southern Rag Medley No. 1: Strains from the Alley" is published by W. B. Allen.

1909 Boone's "Southern Rag Medley No. 2: Strains from Flat Branch" is published by W. B. Allen.

1912 Boone signs contract with QRS Company to make piano rolls.

1916 John Lange dies.

1922 Wayne B. Allen becomes Boone's manager.

1927 Boone dies in Warrensburg on October 4. He is buried in Columbia.

Sources for Quotations

11 Melissa Fuell, *Blind Boone: His Early Life and His Achievements* (Kansas City, MO: Burton Publishing Company, 1915), 24.

14 Jack Batterson, *Blind Boone: Missouri's Ragtime Pioneer* (Columbia, MO: University of Missouri Press, 1998), 25.

20 Blind Boone, interview by Jack Batterson, in *Columbia Missourian* (August 25, 1921): 27.

22, 23 Jack Batterson, *Blind Boone,* 29.

27 Melissa Fuell, *Blind Boone,* 32–33.

32 Ibid., 39.

36 Wayne B. Allen, interview by author, Columbia, MO, 1953-1955.

49 Melissa Fuell, *Blind Boone,* 64.

53 Ibid., 20.

58 Allen, interviews.

60 Jack Batterson, *Blind Boone,* 40.

61 Allen, interviews.

62 Melissa Fuell, *Blind Boone,* 141.

62 Ibid., 142.

69 Ibid., 86.

70 Jack Batterson, *Blind Boone,* 47.

72, 76 Allen, interviews.

78 Melissa Fuell, *Blind Boone,* 181.

78 Allen, interviews.

79 Jack Batterson, *Blind Boone,* 91.

79 Blind Boone interviews, reprinted in *Kansas City Times,* February 6, 1950. Blind Boone archives, Mary Miller Smiser Heritage Library, Warrensburg, Missouri.

79 Allen, interviews.

80 Personal memoirs of Maggie Banta Maddox, courtesy of her daughter, Carolyn Maddox Schaberg.

85 Melissa Fuell, *Blind Boone,* 128–129.

97 Ibid., 128.

100 Jack Batterson, *Blind Boone,* 69

102, 103 Allen, interviews.

SELECTED BIBLIOGRAPHY

Books

Batterson, Jack A. *Blind Boone: Missouri's Ragtime Pioneer.* Columbia, MO: University of Missouri Press, 1998.

Berlin, Edward A. *King of Ragtime: Scott Joplin and His Era.* New York, Oxford: Oxford University Press, 1994.

Fuell, Melissa. *Blind Boone: His Early Life and His Achievements.* Kansas City, MO: Burton Publishing Company, 1915.

Jay, Ricky. *Learned Pigs & Fireproof Women: Unique, Eccentric and Amazing Entertainers.* New York: Villard Books, 1987.

Unpublished Collections

The archives below contain clippings, letters, articles, concert programs, reviews, photographs, and artifacts of Boone's career.

Boone County Historical Society Archive, Walters-Boone County Historical Museum, Columbia, Missouri. Blind Boone collection.

Mary Miller Smiser Heritage Library, Johnson County Historical Society, Warrensburg, Missouri. Blind Boone archives.

State Historical Society of Missouri, Columbia, Missouri. Blind Boone file.

Trails Regional Library, Warrensburg Branch, Warrensburg, Missouri. Blind Boone file.

Western Historical Manuscript Collection, 2 Ellis Library, University of Missouri, Columbia, Missouri. Blind Boone Memorial Foundation, Inc., Papers, 1886–1976.

Website

John William Boone Heritage Foundation
<http://blindboone.missouri.org> (October 10, 2002)

OTHER RESOURCES ON BLIND BOONE AND HIS TIMES

Audio Recordings

Boone, John William "Blind." *Blind Boone's Piano Music: An African American Composer Performed by Frank Townsell.* Laurel Records, 1998. Twelve of Boone's compositions available through Laurel Records, 2451 Nichols Canyon, Los Angeles, CA 90046-1798. Phone: (213) 876-6050. Website: <http://www.alphanet.co.il/franktownsell/order-the-cd.html>

———— *Merit Not Sympathy Wins.* Blind Boone Park, 2001. Boone himself playing seven of his compositions and arrangements, taken from surviving QRS piano rolls, available through the Blind Boone Park Committee, 131 SW 300, Warrensburg, MO 64093. Website: <http://www.blindboonepark.org/donations.htm>

Mattox, Cheryl Warren. *Let's Get the Rhythm of the Band: A Child's Introduction to Music from African-American Culture with History and Song.* Nashville, TN : JTG of Nashville, 1994. A companion book is also available.

Wiggins, Thomas. *John Davis Plays Blind Tom.* Newport Classics, 2000.

Books

Collier, Christopher, and James Lincoln Collier. *Reconstruction and the Rise of Jim Crow, 1864–1896.* New York: Benchmark Books, 2000.

Hansen, Joyce. *Bury Me Not in a Land of Slaves: African-Americans in the Time of Reconstruction.* New York: Franklin Watts, 2000.

Igus, Toyomi. *I See the Rhythm.* San Francisco: Children's Book Press, 1998.

Morgan, Thomas L., and William Barlow. *From Cakewalks to Concert Halls: An Illustrated History of African American Popular Music from 1895 to 1930.* Washington, D.C.: Elliot & Clark Publishing, 1992.

Websites

A Brief History of Blind Boone
<http://www.blindboonepark.org/whoisblindboone.htm>
A summary of Blind Boone's life, this site is an ideal place to begin further study.

John William Boone
<http://www.bocomo.org/blindb.htm>
Historic photos and links to Blind Boone music files make this site a great addition to your learning experience. Listen to the Rag Medleys for a great example of Blind Boone's style.

Musings on Music: Blind Boone
<http://www.janeellen.com/music/blindboone.html>
This site features a catalogue of Blind Boone's compositions along with a short biography.

Ragtime Music of Saint Louis
<http://www.usgennet.org/usa/mo/county/stlouis/ragtime.htm>
Listen to selections of ragtime music from Blind Boone's home state on this site. A brief history of ragtime music accompanies the downloadable songs.

The Styles of Jazz: Ragtime
<http://www.wnur.org/jazz/styles/ragtime/index.html>
This site provides a longer history of ragtime music. Features include a timeline, artist profiles, and quotes about the music from the musicians themselves.

INDEX

Glasgow, MO, 49–50
Gottschalk, Louis Moreau, 58–59, 63
Great Britain, 87

Hayden, Scott, 89
Hendrix, Harrison (stepfather), 21–22,
    44–45, 97; and his five sons (Ed,
    Harry, Ricely, Sam, Tom), 21, 87–88
Hot Springs, AR, 104

J. W. Jenkins & Sons Piano Company,
    69
jazz, 100, 101
Jazz Age, 101
Jeffries, Reverend, 49, 50
Jim Crow, 92–93
Johnson County Courthouse, 18
Johnson, Tom, 47, 48
Joplin, Scott, 88, 89

Kansas City, MO, 84–85
Ku Klux Klan, 17

Lange, Eugenia. *See* Eugenia Boone
Lange, John Jr., 50–53, 61, 62, 75, 84;
    financial support of Boone, 67, 85;
    death, 97; helps Boone launch his
    concert career, 53–55; saves Boone's
    life, 69–70; tours with Boone, 60,
    65–67, 92–93
Lange, Ruth, 52, 65, 68, 82, 84, 96
"Last Dream Waltz," 78
Lee, Reverend John, 50
Lincoln, President Abraham, 16
Liszt, Franz, 59, 72

Maddox, Maggie Banta, 80
"Maple Leaf Rag," 89
Marshall, Arthur, 89
"Marshfield Tornado," 60–63, 103, 104
May, Stella, 65, 68, 88

Missouri School for the Blind, 22–23,
    28–33, 35–36
Morrow, Columbus, 20

Paola, KS, 93–94
piano rolls, 8, 95–96, 102–103
Plessy v. Ferguson, 92

QRS Company, 96

ragtime music, 8, 73, 88, 89, 99–100
Reconstruction, 16–17
recordings of Blind Boone's music, 9,
    117
Reiter, Sam, 42–43

Saint Louis, MO, 27, 33–34
Scott, James, 90–91
segregation, 92–93
Shed, General, 11, 15
"Southern Rag Medley #1: Strains from
    the Alley," 90
"Southern Rag Medley #2: Strains from
    Flat Branch," 90
spirituals, 8, 19, 88
Sting, the, 89

Tenderloin District, Saint Louis, 34–35

Underground Railroad, 14

Vandalia, MO, 44

Warrensburg, MO, 17, 18, 32
"The Whippoorwill," 66–67
White, James Shannon, 94–95

ABOUT THE AUTHOR

Madge Harrah is an award-winning children's book author and playwright. She grew up in Missouri with people who had known Blind Boone personally and had witnessed his spectacular piano performances. She lives in Albuquerque, New Mexico.